A Special Gift

PRESENTED TO

_____

FROM

_____

GRANDMA'S
Christmas Legacy

THE TESTIMONY OF THE TREE

All photos © Jupiter Images unless otherwise noted.
    cover © Rosie Hardy | flickr.com/rosie_hardy
    pages 24-27 © Monika Dembowska | flickr.com/moniqe
    page 44 © Laura Merwin | flickr.com/bayroad

Scriptures are taken from either the *New King James Version* (copyright © 1982 by Thomas
Nelson, Inc., used by permission, all rights reserved) or from *The Message* (copyright © 2002
by NavPress Publishing Group, used by permission, all rights reserved).

Published by W.O.W. Ministries, 540 Lakota Lane, Chaska, MN 55318. You can reach us
on the Internet at www.testimonyofthetree.org and www.wowministriesintl.org

ISBN 13: 978-0-615-30996-5
ISBN 10: 0615309968

Literary development and cover/interior design by Koechel Peterson & Associates, Inc.,
Minneapolis, Minnesota.

Manufactured in China

THIS BOOK IS DEDICATED TO
the true Father of Christmas.

*

Like the star atop the tree
that You would be crowned alone in the radiance
of all your glory to shine on mankind
as the bright and morning star.

*

Like angels announcing good news, faithful friends
and warriors of families championing not just myself but families worldwide
Jen, Deborah, Jennifer, Donna, Katie, Carrie and
Countless others on bended knee before the Christ Child.

*

Like shepherds tending the flocks by night
Marty, my beloved, Mickie, Chris, Isaiah, Jaclyn, and Jen

*

Like the wise men bearing gifts by the wealth of their wisdom
David, Lance, and John, Joyce, Randy and Rebecca

*

All of those who will announce and share the good news
of the birth of the King! Merry Christmas!

GRANDMA'S CHRISTMAS LEGACY

The old gentleman

STOOD IN THE DOORWAY OF HIS MODEST WHITE FARMHOUSE, WITH ITS OLD-FASHIONED GREEN SHUTTERS, STARING OUT THE WINDOW. A GUST OF WIND SHOOK THE DOOR AND RATTLED THE TALL WINDOWS AND SWEPT DOWN AGAIN WITH A MOAN, WHIRLING BIG WHITE SNOWFLAKES OVER EVERYTHING. THE FARMYARD WAS BURIED UNDER WHITE TUFTS AS THE FRESH FALLEN FLAKES GLISTENED LIKE DIAMONDS IN THE LIGHT THAT CASCADED THROUGH THE TREES ACROSS THE SNOWY BLANKET. NESTLED IN THE WARMTH OF THE FARMHOUSE, THE MARTIN FAMILY GATHERED TO SHARE THE ANNUAL TRADITION OF DECORATING THE CHRISTMAS TREE.

Rose Michaels glanced at her father, Christopher Martin, as she cleared space in the corner of the living room for the Christmas tree, preparing the stand. The room was pleasant with its large windows graced with white muslins, comfortable sofa, and pretty rosewood chairs. A bright fire was blazing and crackling in the stone hearth, and its warmth made everything else seem far away.

"Your mother would have loved being here today," Christopher said quietly, almost reverently, as he turned the silver doorknob, opened the wooden door, and took a deep drink of the cool bracing air.

"Grandpa, Grandpa, look!" exclaimed Rose's two children, Grace and Luke, nearly tumbling through the doorway, then stomping the snow from their boots and tossing off gloves and coats at their feet.

As the children exploded in chatter about how cold their noses and fingers were, Rose's husband, James, carried in the healthy evergreen they had cut down in the woods. Taking off his boots, he delivered the promising pine to the corner of the small living room and grunted as he hoisted it into the stand Rose had made ready.

"That's a real beauty," Grandpa Martin said, his voice vibrating with sincerity. "Who picked it out?"

"I did!" seven-year-old Grace reported, kicking her boots off on the braided rug.

"No, Dad did," Luke countered, shaking his head in disgust.

"We all agreed it was the best one," James said as he took off his heavy jacket, tossing it across the back of the rocking chair. "Wow! Does the tree smell good or what?"

"It's incredible," Rose added, breathing in the aroma as she handed James a cup of freshly brewed coffee and kissed him lightly on the forehead.

James took a long sip of the brown steaming brew, staring at the tree. "Do you remember what your mom would always say when we first brought in the Christmas tree and she smelled it?"

Rose nodded and pushed back some loose strands of auburn hair that had fallen across her forehead. Although she smiled, there was no doubting the glance of pain in her deep brown eyes. Her mother had passed away in the late summer, and this was the family's first Christmas without her. She tried to speak but the words caught in her throat.

"No one loved Christmas . . . and the Christmas tree more than your mother," her father chimed in, as Grace took hold of his thick calloused hand. Peering down at his granddaughter, he said, "She'd always say that our lives should be like the freshly cut pine with its sweet fragrance—that no matter where we are, we should be a refreshing fragrance, that others would know who God is through our lives. She'd quote the words the apostle Paul taught: 'Thanks be to God who always leads us in triumphal procession in Christ, and through us spreads everywhere, the fragrance of the knowledge of Him.'"

"That was Mom," Rose added, wiping a tear from her eye. "No matter what shadow fell on her path, she was light; when sorrows rolled in like clouds, she was joy."

"You know," Grandpa said, picking up a long strand of Christmas lights like a lasso and beginning to thread the tree, "it was the strangest thing. That last day just before Grandma left us to be in heaven, she said, 'Christopher, promise me you'll decorate the tree at Christmas, with all our friends and family. Promise me.' And so, we're here today. But I've wondered and wondered why it was her last wish."

"I've asked myself the same question a hundred times," Rose said. "Why was it so important that we do this today?"

"I don't know," Grandpa replied, "but I'm glad we're all here to share it."

Rose grinned in agreement and asked, "Are the Christmas tree decorations in the same spot?"

Grandpa nodded his head. "Yes, in the attic right across from Grandma's writing nook, at least as far as I know. It's been awhile since I've been up there."

"I'll go up and look, and you guys can drink the hot chocolate that's on the stove," Rose said.

Grandpa stayed to finish the lights while James and the grandkids headed for the kitchen. Rose buttoned her heavy woolen sweater and stepped toward the narrow wooden stairway.

"I'll be right back," Rose called out as she ascended the staircase to the second floor, then turned to climb the steeper steps leading to the spacious attic. Opening the narrow door, the creaking hinge announced her entrance into the stillness of the room faintly lit by a single narrow window that cast a soft glow across her mother's writing desk. Notched within the angles of the roofline with its exposed rafters and wide plank floor, the nook was the single spot of solace her mother had found from the daily duty and noisy bustle of farm life. Here she would attend her private passion of writing poetry or letters in the early morning or late evening hours.

Stepping inside the cool attic, she suddenly felt she had stepped back in time. Staring at the desk, it was as if the flooding of light through the window made manifest the memories of the loving mother she so cherished. As vividly as if it were just yesterday, she remembered as a young girl sitting and reading in a small wooden chair next to her mother as she would write. Distinct memories of her mother's heart being poured out on page flooded her mind like a wave and overflowed as tears, which she tried to blink away.

Realizing the distraction and that the family was waiting downstairs, Rose stepped toward the storage boxes in the opposite corner of the room to retrieve the tree decorations. Yet oddly, there in front of the Christmas decor was a small antique trunk she had never seen before. "Where did this come from?" she whispered into the crisp air.

Kneeling beside the trunk, she traced her fingers along its edge and studied its intricate metalwork. Then came the sudden realization. "This is it!" She gasped. "Whatever is in here is the reason why she wants us to be here today."

Elated with anticipation, Rose carefully lifted the trunk and quickly exited the room. Maneuvering the cumbersome find back down the stairway, she made her way into the living room, then set the chest in front of the fireplace next to the bare tree. "Everybody, come in here!" she called out, still staring at the spectacle in wonderment.

Grace came running out of the kitchen, with a slight chocolate mustache and a bright smile. "What's that?" she asked as the others followed behind her. "Is that Grandma's?"

Grandpa, having just plugged in the lights on the tree, turned to see the commotion and said, "Yes, that's Grandma's trunk. It belonged to her grandmother. Her brother gave it to her early last spring."

"No wonder I've never seen it," Rose responded. "It was placed right in front of the Christmas decorations. Dad, is this why we are here today?"

Luke and Grace plopped down beside the trunk.

"Maybe there are Christmas presents from Grandma!" Luke exclaimed.

12

"Something nostalgic?" James sounded.

"No," Grandpa said with conviction as he struggled to crouch beside the trunk, "knowing Grandma, she had something more important in mind."

Taking a deep breath, then exhaling slowly to compose herself, Rose said, "Let's find out." She reached down, unfastened the locks, lifted the lid, and peered inside. Her lips curled into an unconscious smile, and her eyes brightened. "Oh my goodness! A Christmas card, and can you believe it, there's a velvet book and a box beneath it."

Everyone moved closer, crowding the trunk, and gazed silently, even reverently, at the sweet mystery that Grandma had hidden away for this very moment. There beneath the handmade card and velvet covered book was an open box of ornaments hand painted with care, nesting patiently on a bed of lace-like garland.

"I knew she was up to something," Grandpa said. Reaching in, he lifted out the card, grateful to hold just one more thing graced by her. The hand drawn cover revealed a single, small, forlorn looking evergreen tree, alone in the snowy drifts. "I should have looked there. She spent a lot of time in her nook in the early spring. I can't read this. I'll choke up. James, can you?"

James reached for the card. Together they snuggled in around the trunk, now a treasure chest discovered. Viewing the simple sketch of the barren little pine, deprived of most of its needles and leaning from the elements, James opened it, studied the words for several seconds, then glanced lovingly at Rose. Taking a deep breath, he started to read:

Dear Ones,

Last year on Christmas Eve, I knew I may not be sharing this Christmas with you. So it was then, after all were in bed, I sat to reflect beside the warm fire within the glow of the Christmas tree. I bowed my head and asked God to provide a gift—a means for you and those who shall follow to know the grace that I have found, giving purpose to your lives and to your families. Something that would stand the test of time, helping you transcend loss and fear and bringing hope for both the good times and the bad.

And so, while in the quiet as I bowed my head, I felt a deep presence of immense peace. Looking up, suddenly, it was there, standing right before me—glistening and adorned in all of its glory was the answer, a gift.

In all the years of decorating and crowning it with the star, I never realized this tree stood as a symbol of all we are to know and all we are to be. It was then the revelation was clear of what I was to do. So through the months before I weaken, I pen these pages and prepare the contents of this trunk.

Find here now, the book beneath, a lesson—a Christmas custom—I wish to pass to you. Together learn what I have seen, for amongst the branches of this promising pine are lessons of life and love to unfold. There you will find promise and hope to carry you through the years. This is my prayer, a legacy for you, that you may stand as a symbol of hope in a dark world, adorned in strength and beauty as does the tree a testament. For this is our testimony. This is the testimony of the tree.

Love, Grandma

"Unbelievable . . ." James finally said, closing the card and setting it back down beside the trunk. Then he carefully lifted the handmade velvet book out of the trunk, revealing all that rested beneath for inspection. There an open box of nine beautifully hand painted ornaments and a gold leaf star lay patiently on a bed of snowy white tulle as if resting on a cloud, no doubt the work of her hands.

"This is such a mystery. Why this?" Grandpa asked.

Leaning on his father's arm, Luke stroked his little fingers across the handbound book covered with scraps of velvet. "It's so soft," he whispered.

Slowly opening the cover, James lifted out a large sprig of pine, the sweet odor suddenly permeating the air.

"I smell Christmas!" Grace whispered.

"She remembered," Grandpa said with a chuckle.

Rose laughed and cried at the same time. "She did. She wanted to remind us again of the fragrance of our lives."

James turned some of the pages of the book. "Do you want me to read it now?"

"Yes," Rose answered, her cheeks flushed with emotion. "Is it handwritten?"

James nodded. "It is penned in her beautiful script." He held the book up for them to see. The title page clearly read *The Testimony of the Tree*. Then he turned the book around, opened to the first page, and began to read:

Christmas, the season of hope and goodwill, when a dark world pauses to ponder the "why" of our past year and the "what" of our future. We seek a glimmer of hope to refresh us, and all because of the glory that shone from one lone babe born in the cold of the same dark world—Jesus, the Christ Child, the light and hope of the world.

Yet in the midst of the busyness of the celebration of the holiday, can this hope still be found? Can it be at the center of our buying, our doing, our gathering with feasts and festivals, as stands the Christmas tree in the center of our homes? The answer is before you.

The simple evergreen, although unadorned, is fragrant and no less beautiful. What makes for such beauty is its color of green. Of course, green represents life . . . new life. It reminds us that God's Book, the Bible, tells the true Christmas story of how a baby boy was born in Bethlehem, yet this was not any child. It says the child's mother, Mary, was a virgin. His birth was a miracle of God. The angel sent to Mary told her, "Call His name Immanuel," which means "God with us." This was the Father God's plan for us—not just to believe but to know Him, to have a relationship with Him as God among us.

Yet there is more that sets the Christmas tree apart. It is an "evergreen"— the same in and out of season, in contrast to other trees that change color, drop their leaves, and are dormant for the winter. Similarly, Jesus is the same yesterday, today, and forever, and He says to us, "I will never leave you nor forsake you." He is the Alpha and the Omega, the beginning and the end, the everlasting God, who is always with us. That's God's everlasting covenant, or binding promise, with us. When I look at a Christmas tree, it reminds me that nothing can ever separate me from the love of God. That gives me hope straight into eternity. What a great reminder and gift of hope at Christmas!

"Are you, okay, Grandpa?" Luke broke in, glancing up and staring into his grandfather's clear brown eyes. "Grandma means she's in heaven, right?"

Grandpa just nodded, the loneliness of the past months being too much to hide. Taking a deep breath, he said, "Yes, she is . . . and I miss her dearly. We all do. But keep reading, James."

James's face was flushed by the exchange, and his eyes seemed to strain a bit to see Grandma's handwritten script more clearly.

So this is what the simple and unadorned green pine represents to us. That new life came in the simplest and most humble form— an innocent babe born in a lowly manger. Time would reveal his destiny as the plan for all mankind. He was born to die as a sacrifice for us and our sins, that through the forgiveness of sin we too would have this new life.

The Bible as God's love letter tells us, "For God so loved the world that He gave His only begotten Son, that whoever believes in Him should not perish but have everlasting life." What an incredible, special gift! Jesus, the only Son of God, came to this dark world so we could have new life, God's life in us. Jesus promised, "I have come that they may have life, and that they may have it more abundantly." So this tree represents a person who is a follower of Jesus, someone who has received that new life and has it abundantly here on earth right now. We don't have to wait for heaven.

WHEN I LOOK AT A CHRISTMAS TREE,

it reminds me that nothing can ever

separate me from the love of God.

Yet I saw something else in the branches of the Christmas tree. Just as there are many, many branches on the tree, there are many parts to our lives. For instance, we may be a father, a son, a mother, or a daughter. We have our thought lives and how we think about ourselves. Other branches include our careers, our relationships, our plans, our hopes, and our dreams. Like boughs of the pine tree, there are numerous aspects to our lives.

But when you look at a Christmas tree, it's not perfect. Some branches are flourishing, while others are sparse and bare of green. A few may be short, while others are long; some look out of place and off-kilter. And some are completely missing altogether, leaving a gaping hole on one side. Although misshapen, it's still a Christmas tree despite its flaws. How much is that like our own lives? Even though we believe in God, our lives are far from perfect. There are areas of our lives that are sticking out of place, perhaps damaged, or lacking altogether.

So what do we do about that? God invites each of us to do what the three wise men did. They were led by a star to Bethlehem to find the foretold King of kings and Lord of lords. They bowed and worshiped the infant Jesus, giving gifts to honor this King. Even though they were from different backgrounds, different countries, and different faiths, they knew as foreign rulers or priests that Jesus Christ was the Son of the living God, the one true God, Jehovah.

So what can we do? Take each area of our lives and humbly bow them in submission to Jesus as Lord, laying down all before Him as the wise men did. In humility, we recognize that all we have and all we are comes from God. Humble people put their focus on God and what He has done for us, rather than on themselves and their accomplishments. Humility shapes our lives in a way that points people to Christ. While we acknowledge that we are inadequate and sinful, it leads to an exalting and praising of God.

The Psalmist said, "The LORD raises those who are bowed down; the LORD loves the righteous." God promises that when we give every area of our lives to Jesus, like the lowering boughs of the pine, only then can we take on the true and proper shape we were meant to have—and that is one that points others to God.

Jesus said these very words, "I am the way, the truth, and the life. No one comes to the Father except through Me." He is our only hope for salvation. Before we put our trust in Him, God describes our lives this way: "A life devoted to things is a dead life, a stump." Once we come to know Jesus, the description changes to "a God-shaped life is a flourishing tree."

Grace leaned forward and said, "We saw a lot of dead stumps in the woods this morning . . . and some gigantic trees."

"Would you like to be a stump or a tree, honey?" James asked with a knowing smile.

"I want to be the biggest, tallest, most beautiful tree in the woods!" Grace responded, motioning with airy waves of her hands.

"That's sort of what Grandma meant," James replied, glancing down at the manuscript. "Looks like she has more to say about it."

Amazingly, when we humble our lives and make Jesus our Lord, then God gives us another promise—"a great reward." Like ornaments gracing branches bowed low on the tree, He takes each area we relinquish before Him and He adorns them, decorating our lives with gifting and gracing. Each applied in turn will transform our hearts, minds, and even our souls, bringing strength and adding beauty to our lives. So as a lesson and a legacy, I have made these ornaments for you to adorn the tree as you follow along.

LOVE

Rose then peered within the trunk, taking out the first ornament. She handed the red-burnished bulb carefully to Grace, her eyes wide with wonder.

"Love," Grace said as she read the paint strokes of her grandmother's gift. Hanging it on the tree, her father continued to read:

> The first ornament that God gives us is His unconditional Love, as is supremely expressed in Jesus coming to die for us on the cross. His love for us is completely undeserved, and His grace and love give us the ability to love and forgive others despite what they may be like. The apostle Paul said, "And now abide faith, hope, love, these three; but the greatest of these is love." When we love, it makes our faith strong. And when others love us, it gives us hope. Just think of the hope we can bring to someone else if we forgive them!

And this brings the second gift, Joy, to our lives, which is a gladness in our heart and soul that remains undimmed by the trials, tests, and tribulations facing our lives. Although we live in a world filled with apathy, hurts, and uncertainty, the Psalmist said that in God's presence is "fullness of joy." When we welcome His presence into our lives, we experience His joy, and it becomes our strength. We can then share that joy with others.

The adornment that follows Joy is Peace. Before the birth of Jesus, shepherds were in the fields watching their flocks by night, and what happened? A mighty host of angels came praising God and saying, "Glory to God in the highest, and on earth peace, goodwill toward men!" Our Father God planned for us to have peace within despite the dark world. This is part of His goodwill toward mankind. Peace does not mean that our lives are free from troubles, but is a deep assurance in our soul—a contentment that allows us to enjoy all of God's gifts and blessings because of the deposit of God's joy in our hearts. And it extends out through our lives to bring this "peace and goodwill to all men."

What comes from Peace? It's Patience or Longsuffering. Notice these adornments are not only principles to apply, but they are sequential. Can you have patience or longsuffering without peace? When Love, Joy, and Peace have proper place in your life, Patience will follow as the fruit. God will gift you with an attitude that never loses hope for others, even if they provoke and attack you. Patience refuses to surrender to circumstances, difficulties, or criticism.

From the adornment of Peace applied, Kindness or Tenderhearted Care comes and puts others at ease and shrinks from giving pain. The Word of God states that "when the kindness and the love of God our Savior toward man appeared . . . He saved us." It was the tender love of Jesus that softened our hearts, wiped away our apathy, and won us to faith. Our kindness extended is a bridge to others that God's love may pass over. And it is His kindness that leads all to repentance. God decorates us with His kindness so that others may know Him and know Him more fully.

fruit of
THE SPIRIT

GENTLENESS
longsuffering

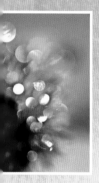

"Luke is mean to me," Grace piped in, flashing her green eyes at her brother. "He shoved me into a snow bank and then wiped my face with snow."

"Because she smacked me in the ear with an ice ball yesterday," Luke retorted, "and it felt like it ripped my ear off. I wanted to—"

"Which means we all have to learn to practice kindness, right?" Rose interrupted. "Remember what we teach in our family: Every act we do has a decision attached to it. We must place these ornaments on ourselves every day. That is what practice means here."

Grace lit up like the Christmas tree and said, "I guess that after God helps us to put these ornaments on, we can let them fall right off."

"Then we won't look pretty anymore," Luke assessed.

"That's right," Rose said, then nodded to James to keep reading.

Goodness is next as good works flow from a kind heart. As kindness is an open hand extended, so goodness is a hand in action that gives a hand up. The goodness of God desires to give others what was never deserved—generously, liberally, with an open hand. We are encouraged to "spur one another on to good works," not for the sake of earning what we cannot buy—our salvation—instead, that we might freely reflect this beautiful characteristic of God in our lives as a testament to others.

TENDERHEARTED

Goodness leads to Faithfulness, a faithful life, in the same way that God is faithful to us. A faithful person is someone we can depend upon and whose word we can trust unreservedly. And when you see people who are truly faithful, you'll see that they have the favor of God on their lives, because faithfulness brings the fullness of God's blessing and favor.

Higher on the tree and harder to reach is the next principle of Gentleness or Meekness. From a faithful life comes a maturity that brings the quiet strength of Gentleness, which is comparable to a horse that has been trained and is obedient to the reins. It is the power through which the Holy Spirit harnesses the strong and explosive might of our passions and desires and uses them for the good of all. Gentleness has power. It is the quiet strength of Christ.

Finally, the last adornment is Self-control. This is how we steer away from temptations. It gives us the strength of character to restrain ourselves from doing wrong. And isn't it interesting that it's the last one? You see, you can't have Self-control if you don't have Gentleness, or Faithfulness, or Goodness, or Kindness, or Patience, or Peace, or Joy. Why? Because they are all are rooted in the first one, which is Love.

Kindness

And so now we are adorned. Submitting every aspect of our lives to God not only allows Him to adorn us with the beauty of His character, it invites His Holy Spirit's presence to be woven throughout every area of our lives. These principles applied bring the outcome and fruit of the Spirit transforming us into the likeness of Christ.

I love this promise God gives us: "He has clothed me with the garments of salvation, He has covered me with the robe of righteousness, as a bridegroom decks himself with ornaments, and as a bride adorns herself with her jewels." As the groom and bride adorn themselves, we are called to adorn our lives. Yet although now adorned, He in preparation now dresses us with even more beauty. We too can be dressed and covered in preparation with the beauty of the Lord.

As the lace-like garland is woven amongst the branches of the Christmas tree, the One weaving and wrapping His presence throughout our lives is called "the breath of God," the Holy Spirit. He was sent to move through every area of our lives with His presence, to wrap us with His care and comfort, and to grace us with the promise of His power and provision that we may be prepared to live out our purpose in Him.

Grace lifted the fluffy tulle from the trunk, wrapped it around her shoulders, and announced, "Daddy, look, I am covered and safe like when we pray at bedtime, and I know God is with us."

"Yes," James responded, "and He adorns and covers you with all you need to point others to Jesus as does the tree. That's why these ornaments are called 'the fruit of the Spirit.' He gives you the right heart, the right attitude, and even the right words when you don't know what to say."

Luke had a quizzical look on his face. "Did Grandma mean we are supposed to tell other people this story about the Christmas tree?"

"She did . . ." James said slowly as if it was just dawning on him as well, "because she wanted us to know how the Holy Spirit prepares us. The reason He 'dresses and adorns us' is to show us His heart of love and care not just for us, but also for others. He takes away our indifference and apathy and changes us to be like Jesus and Grandma, desiring others to know the love of God forever."

Rose added for the children, "Just think of the difference we can make in the lives of others . . . in the lives of entire families, when we show and shine with the love of God like the tree."

"Grandma has more to say about that," James said, glancing back down at the book and starting to read again.

So as the pinnacle adornment of this pine, crowning all that the tree is and represents, we place the star atop the tree symbolizing, first and foremost, that Jesus would be the pinnacle of our lives— the sovereign Lord over all of who we are. Jesus is "the bright and morning star." His desire is to shine over us with His protection, on us with His gracing, in us with the light of His power, and through us with His gifting. It is then the display is complete for all to behold. We were born to worship Him, and this is why He came. So the star is a symbol of His glory and manifest presence shining over, on, in, and through us.

And as we light the Christmas tree, we're reminded that like the numerous lights gracing each branch, the many good works we offer should shine and emanate from every part of our lives, illuminating the great love and goodness of God. Jesus said, "Let your light so shine before men, that they may see your good works and glorify your Father in heaven." We are to stand as a symbol of hope in a dark world, as does the Christmas tree, a display of His goodness and greatness, to radiate the glory of God.

Allow the Holy Spirit to work all of this in your life, and the beauty of the Lord will shine through your life and point others to the way of the Christ Child.

With the sunlight now dimming across the western sky, within the farmhouse the tree's twinkling lights illuminated the story's message even more. They paused, taken aback by the newfound meaning of the Christmas tree.

Raising his eyes from the text, James spoke with a grin, "She's not done." Picking up the Christmas card, he handed it to Rose and said, "Pass this around as I finish the last bit." Rose studied the little tree, left to stand in the snowy elements, weathered and worn, deprived of most of its needles yet trying to hold onto its many pinecones. As the family peered over her shoulders at the straggly and bare pine, James continued.

Not everyone feels this way—beautiful and adorned. Look at the card. This small sprig left to the elements of the cold world needs the loving touch of the Master, too. It is not tall and true; its trunk is twisted and made crooked by the elements. It is not adorned in purpose. Although not young, it is still nearly as small as a seedling. Alone it stands. So we are without knowing our Creator. We are born, there is life, yet it is not marked by eternal life.

People can feel the same way, too—depleted, with unexplained loneliness, left with little purpose. Some, due to their stormy environment, feel rejected and worn. Life has caused them to grow crooked; their beauty and potential has not been realized. Nevertheless, there is hope. The Word of God says, "The LORD takes pleasure in His people; He will beautify the humble with salvation."

Look at this lifeless tree and consider again Jesus' words, "I have come that they may have life, and that they may have it more abundantly." Do you notice the one thing that's left on this tree that the storms of life cannot remove? The pinecones, which are the seeds. Your specific gifts and the gracing He has for you are represented by the many pinecones.

God, the Creator of all things, even the Creator of creativity itself, before the foundations of the world, shaped the "who" of you and me. He placed the many seeds of His gifting and gracing within us, the very plans of our destiny. They proclaim the hidden potential that the seeds of your gifting may grow.

God says, "For I know the plans that I have for you, declares the Lord, plans to prosper you and not harm you. Plans to give you a hope and future. And when you come to me, and when you pray to me and seek me with all of your heart, I will be found by you, declares the Lord."

Do you know how a pinecone releases its seeds? It's only when it is totally dry or when it is consumed by fire. Isn't that amazing? So there is a message of hope for us.

This tree represents who I was before I put my faith in Christ. When my parents divorced, I felt so much shame, so worthless, and a failure for not being able to hold them together. I felt crooked, dry, and beaten. Although I believed that God was real and that His love was sacrificial, I didn't believe that He could love me. So this is how I stood until someone told me the good news about God's unconditional love. My earnest desire for you and all who will follow is that you know God's love, no matter what you've experienced in your life. Because "a life devoted to things is a dead life, a stump; a God-shaped life is a flourishing tree."

And that is where I must end my story, my loved ones. My prayer for you and for all those with whom you share the "Testimony of the Tree" is that you may stand as this promising pine to tell of the greatness and goodness of God the Father through His plan revealed—the hope and salvation brought through His Son Jesus, and the Spirit-led life realized by the gifting and gracing of the Holy Spirit. This is my prayer, a legacy for you. That you may stand as a symbol of hope in a dark world, adorned in strength and beauty, just as the tree stands as a testament. For this is our testimony . . . the testimony of the tree.

James slowly closed the handmade velvet book. Looking up, together they gazed upon the tree, their thoughts suspended in the words they'd just read. Then he spoke softly, "I'll never see the Christmas tree the same way again."

"Now I understand this is a call and purpose for our whole family," Rose noted.

Grace chimed in, "Can this be our new Christmas tradition?"

"Absolutely, but how do we start?" Rose asked.

"First with ourselves, then with all we know," James answered with conviction.

Just then, the doorbell rang, and Grace and Luke jumped up and raced to the door.

"It's the neighbors," Luke called out.

Grandma had requested that they would decorate the tree not only with their family but with all of their friends as well, and having received Grandpa's invitation, they were right on time.

And so began the tradition of *Grandma's Christmas Legacy, the Testimony of the Tree.*

"Today, If You Hear His Voice . . ."

As the tree stood before you, did you hear the message? Do you hear God's voice inviting you to the life abundant in Jesus Christ? Do you wish for the new life reflected in the tall, adorned tree?

The story of the Christmas tree is a gift. Yet the greatest gift our Father in heaven could have ever given also came on a tree. You see, it was on a cross made from cedar planks of pine that Jesus gave us the greatest gift—His life. As the Christmas tree, the planks of pine that made the cross also tell a story.

Jesus came as "God with us" to this fallen world ridden with sin and "dwelt among us." God's love letter to us states, "For all have sinned and fallen short of the glory of God." He was the perfect one in an imperfect world. He was born to die on a tree where our shame and scorn could be placed upon Him.

The horizontal beam of the cross represents Jesus' life as a man, mortal here on earth. Behold Jesus as He spread His hands out and said to us, "I love you. I love you this much." There was nothing of beauty hung there, only the ugliness of our sin. The One from the wooden manger now dies on a wooden cross, taking on the sin of all mankind and the penalty of death for us all.

The vertical part of the cross represents where heaven above came down and invaded earth. Where the cross was plunged into the earth, that rocky hill was called "Golgotha," translated "the place of the skull," meaning death. Yet look at the cross again. Do you see? It is shaped as a sword, and Jesus is truth—the very sword of truth. Plunging down from heaven and piercing through the very symbol of death and reaching to the very depths of hell and Hades, Jesus defeated and killed death itself through the cross. For after bearing the penalty for sin, He was resurrected, proving His Lordship over sin and death. "O death, where is your victory; o death, where is your sting?" As the Lord of life, Jesus is the Lord triumphant over death and over all.

This Christmas, behold the manger and beyond—
- Behold the cross, the tree of Calvary, the sword piercing death that we might live.
- Behold the Savior hung upon it, the truth of our salvation.
- Behold the risen Christ, the light and hope of the world.

An invitation is extended . . .

Today, you may be a follower of Jesus Christ, but perhaps there are certain areas of your life that are lacking like a misshapen tree. Perhaps you need to yield parts of your life, such as pride or selfishness, in true submission to His Lordship. Ask Him to reveal these to you. As you surrender these in relinquishment as the wise men did, ask God for the gifting and gracing of His Holy Spirit to adorn these submitted areas. The most precious Christmas moments are those when God wraps us with His presence to change and transform us. Pray to the Father, the Creator of all things, the Giver of all good things, "Lord, I present all to you. Bring your grace and goodness over me, over my home, and over my family this Christmas. Bring your Holy Spirit to wrap my life that I may more greatly reflect the glory and the image of Jesus. That I may stand in the purpose You have for me."

And if you don't know Jesus personally, you can receive the gift of Jesus Christ as your personal Lord and Savior. Just bow your head and pray, "Father, I thank You that You are real and that You are Lord. Thank You, Jesus, for coming to earth to live and die for me, rising from the dead and proving You are King of kings. Lord, in Jesus' name, please forgive my sins and cleanse my heart. Thank You that You are making me new. I yield everything in my life to You and commit myself to living according to Your will and way. I give You my heart, I give You my soul. Please come and take over my life. And, Lord, I ask that Your Holy Spirit would be evident in my life. I pray for further gracing and gifting of all You are. All glory to You. In Jesus' name, amen."

THE BIRTH OF JESUS

LUKE 2

IN THOSE DAYS Caesar Augustus issued a decree that a census should be taken of the entire Roman world. (This was the first census that took place while Quirinius was governor of Syria.) And everyone went to his own town to register.

So Joseph also went up from the town of Nazareth in Galilee to Judea, to Bethlehem the town of David, because he belonged to the house and line of David. He went there to register with Mary, who was pledged to be married to him and was expecting a child. While they were there, the time came for the baby to be born, and she gave birth to her firstborn, a son. She wrapped him in cloths and placed him in a manger, because there was no room for them in the inn.

And there were shepherds living out in the fields nearby, keeping watch over their flocks at night. An angel of the Lord appeared to them, and the glory of the Lord shone around them, and they were terrified. But the angel said to them, "Do not be afraid. I bring you good news of great joy that will be for all the people. Today in the town of David a Savior has been born to you; he is Christ the Lord. This will be a sign to you: You will find a baby wrapped in cloths and lying in a manger."

Suddenly a great company of the heavenly host appeared with the angel, praising God and saying, "Glory to God in the highest, and on earth peace to men on whom his favor rests."

When the angels had left them and gone into heaven, the shepherds said to one another, "Let's go to Bethlehem and see this thing that has happened, which the Lord has told us about."

So they hurried off and found Mary and Joseph, and the baby, who was lying in the manger. When they had seen him, they spread the word concerning what had been told them about this child, and all who heard it were amazed at what the shepherds said to them. But Mary treasured up all these things and pondered them in her heart. The shepherds returned, glorifying and praising God for all the things they had heard and seen, which were just as they had been told.

On the eighth day, when it was time to circumcise him, he was named Jesus, the name the angel had given him before he had been conceived.

When the time of their purification according to the Law of Moses had been completed, Joseph and Mary took him to Jerusalem to present him to the Lord (as it is written in the Law of the Lord, "Every firstborn male is to be consecrated to the Lord"), and to offer a sacrifice in keeping with what is said in the Law of the Lord: "a pair of doves or two young pigeons."

Now there was a man in Jerusalem called Simeon, who was righteous and devout. He was waiting for the consolation of Israel, and the Holy Spirit was upon him. It had been revealed to him by the Holy Spirit that he would not die before he had seen the Lord's Christ. Moved by the Spirit, he went into the temple courts. When the parents brought in the child Jesus to do for him what the custom of the Law required, Simeon took him in his arms and praised God, saying:

"Sovereign Lord, as you have promised,
you now dismiss your servant in peace.
For my eyes have seen your salvation,
which you have prepared in the sight of all people,
a light for revelation to the Gentiles
and for glory to your people Israel."

The child's father and mother marveled at what was said about him. Then Simeon blessed them and said to Mary, his mother: "This child is destined to cause the falling and rising of many in Israel, and to be a sign that will be spoken against, so that the thoughts of many hearts will be revealed. And a sword will pierce your own soul too."

There was also a prophetess, Anna, the daughter of Phanuel, of the tribe of Asher. She was very old; she had lived with her husband seven years after her marriage, and then was a widow until she was eighty-four. She never left the temple but worshiped night and day, fasting and praying. Coming up to them at that very moment, she gave thanks to God and spoke about the child to all who were looking forward to the redemption of Jerusalem.

When Joseph and Mary had done everything required by the Law of the Lord, they returned to Galilee to their own town of Nazareth. And the child grew and became strong; he was filled with wisdom, and the grace of God was upon him.

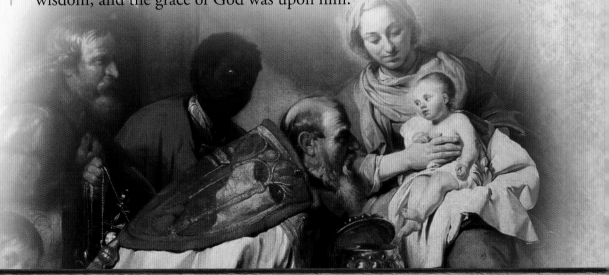

Family
Read-Along
Version

Christmas is celebrated around the world with a rich array of traditions. Isn't it interesting when we look at all the decorations of Christmas, they have stories and meaning behind them—the wreath speaks of hospitality, the candy cane reflects the shepherd's staff, and the stocking symbolizes providing for those without. Yet the largest icon of all is featured prominently in our homes and has been given virtually no meaning—the Christmas tree, and it stands to tell the greatest story of all . . .

The Christmas Tree. Standing in nature's form, not dressed or adorned, the simple green and fragrant pine is the greatest symbol of Christmas. But why? It represents life . . . new life. It reminds me of the Christmas story told in God's book, the Bible, of how a little baby boy was born in Bethlehem. Yet this was not just any child, it says that the child's mother, Mary, was a virgin. His birth was a miracle of God. The angel told Mary, "Call His name Immanuel," which means "God with us." He was Jesus, the Christ ("the Anointed One"), the hope and light of the world. God's story also tells us, "For God so loved the world that he gave his one and only Son, that whoever believes in him shall not perish but have eternal life." So this is what the unadorned green pine represents to us. That new life came in the simplest and most humble form—an innocent babe born in a lowly manger, whose destiny was to reveal His purpose and plan for all mankind. He was born to die as a sacrifice for us and our sins, which the Father cannot look upon, that by the forgiveness of sin, we too would have this new life. What an incredible, special gift! Jesus, the only Son of God, came to this dark world so we could have new life, God's life in us. So this tree represents a person who is a follower of Jesus, someone who has received that new life.

Evergreen. The Christmas tree is an "evergreen." While the maples, oaks, and birches change color, drop their leaves, and are dormant through the winter, the evergreen stands in contrast as the same in and out of season. It is "ever-green" or "ever-lasting." There are three hidden truths to be found here as symbolic in this promising pine. *First,* we discover through the pages of the Bible that God is everlasting. Jesus Christ is the same yesterday, today, and forever. God is the Alpha and the Omega, the beginning and the end. God is everlasting. *Second,* He is always with us. Jesus said, "I will never leave you nor forsake you." That's God's everlasting covenant or binding promise with us. So the Christmas tree reminds us that nothing can ever separate us from the love of God. The *third* everlasting truth is that the evergreen stands as emblem to the specific promise that if we believe in Jesus and have made Him the Lord of our lives, God will grant us everlasting life with Him in heaven. We will not live merely the short life of this "season" on earth as the other seasonal trees, but we will be "ever-green" or "ever-lasting." And that brings us hope, straight into eternity. We now can stand, as the flourishing evergreen tree, with the promise of a healthy life—full, abundant, *and* eternal.

The Branches. When we go to select our Christmas tree, it is hard to find one that is perfect. Some branches are flourishing while others are sparse of green. A few may be short, while others are long, protruding proudly upward and looking out of place and off-kilter. And some branches are completely missing, leaving a gaping hole to one side. Nevertheless, even with its flaws, it's still a Christmas tree. How much is that like our lives? Just as there are many, many branches on the tree, there are many aspects to our lives. For instance, our thought life and how we think about ourselves—our personal identity—may represent one branch. Another may be our careers, our hobbies, or our free time. A branch could be our relationships or our role as a father, mother, son, or daughter. Also, we have our plans, our hopes, and dreams. Together these make up who we are. Yet like the pine waiting to be decked and adorned, we too can have parts of our lives that are a little out of place, damaged, lacking altogether, or lofty and raised in pride. We too are far from perfect. So what do we do?

God invites each of us to do what the three wise men did. They were led by a star to Bethlehem and worshiped the infant Jesus in the manger. Even though they were from different backgrounds, different countries, and different faiths, they all knew as foreign rulers or priests that Jesus Christ was the Son of the living God, the one true God, Jehovah. Finding Him, they bowed to worship the infant Jesus, giving gifts to acknowledge and honor this King of all kings. Like the lowered boughs of the pine create a perfect arrow pointing to the heavens, we can lower the lofty areas of our lives and submit them to His Lordship. In humility, we recognize that all we have and all we are come from the goodness of God. Humble people put their focus on God and what He has done for them, rather than on themselves and their accomplishments. Humility shapes our lives in a way that points people to Christ.

The Psalmist said, "The Lord raises those who are bowed down; the Lord loves the righteous." God promises that when every area of our lives is submitted and relinquished before Him, we will take on the true and proper shape our lives were meant to have—and that is a life that points others to God and His salvation just as the pine with its lowered branches.

Jesus said these very words, "I am the way, the truth, and the life. No one comes to the Father except through Me." Jesus is our only hope for salvation, and we are to point the way to Him. Before we put our trust in Him, God describes our lives this way: "A life devoted to things is a dead life, a stump." Once we come to know Jesus, the description changes to "a God shaped life is a flourishing tree."

So the Christmas tree tells us that as we bow and relinquish each part of our lives to God, He promises to grace and adorn us with a gift—the beauty of Him. And the first ornament that God graces on the tips of the lowered branches of our lives is His . . .

Love. *(Place an ornament on a branch.)* God's unconditional love, as is supremely expressed in Jesus' coming to die for us on the cross, is completely undeserved, and His grace and love in our lives give us the ability to love and forgive others despite what they may be like— an unconditional and sacrificial love like His. "Now abide faith, hope, love, these three; but the greatest of these is love." When we love, it makes our faith strong. And when others love us, it gives us hope. Just think of the hope you can bring to someone else if you forgive them! And this brings the second . . . *(Place an ornament.)*

Joy is gladness in our heart and soul that remains undimmed by the trials, tests, and tribulations we face in our world. Although we live in a world filled with apathy, hurts, uncertainty, and darkness, the Psalmist said that in God's presence is the "fullness of joy." When we welcome His presence into each area of our lives, we experience His joy, and it becomes our strength. We then can share this joy with others, despite our circumstances, because Jesus is the fountain of joy and the wellspring of life.

Peace. *(Place an ornament.)* Before the birth of Jesus, shepherds were in the fields watching their flocks by night, and what happened? A mighty host of angels came praising God and announcing, "Glory to God in the highest, and on earth peace, goodwill toward men!" God's plan is for us to have His peace. Peace does not mean that our lives are free from troubles, but is an assured quietness of soul that allows us to enjoy all of God's gifts and blessings. And it extends out through our lives to bring peace to others. Once we are decorated with Peace . . .

Patience will follow. *(Place an ornament.)* When Love, Joy, and Peace have proper place in our lives, His lasting patience or longsuffering will follow as fruit. He will gift us with an attitude that never loses hope for others despite their actions. Patience refuses to surrender to circumstances, difficulties, or criticism. Patience empowers us with the ability to have true . . .

Kindness, which puts others at ease and shrinks from giving pain. *(Place an ornament.)* The Word of God states that "when the kindness and the love of God our Savior toward man appeared—He saved us." It was the tender love of Jesus that softened our hearts, wiped away our apathy, and won us to faith. God decorates us with His kindness so that others may know Him.

Goodness is next as good works flow from a kind heart. *(Place an ornament.)* The Bible tells us "that the goodness of God leads you to repentance." God's goodness consists of His kindness, grace, righteousness, holiness, justice, mercy, and love. It is the quality of life that desires to give others what was never deserved—generously, liberally, with an open hand. We are encouraged to spur one another on in good works that we might reflect the beautiful character of God in our lives. Goodness in our hearts leads to a life marked by . . .

Faithfulness. *(Place an ornament.)* In the same way that God is faithful to us, a faithful person is someone we can depend upon and whose word we can trust always, unreservedly. And when you see people who are truly faithful, you'll see that they have the favor of God on their life, because faithfulness brings the fullness of God's favor and blessing. . . . Higher on the tree and harder to reach is the next principle applied . . .

Gentleness or Meekness. *(Place an ornament.)* Faithfulness brings a maturity and discipline into our lives that is comparable to a horse that has been trained and is obedient to the reins. From this, we are decorated with a quiet strength. It is the power through which the Holy Spirit harnesses the strong and explosive might of our passions and uses them for the good of all. Gentleness is the opposite of pride. Gentleness gives us the ability to be temperate and gentle in even the hardest situations. We all need that! This power of gentleness or meekness gives us the ability to steer away from temptations, bringing us . . .

Self-Control. *(Place an ornament.)* This last ornament adorns our lives with the strength of character to restrain from doing wrong. God's instruction manual, the Bible, says that "all have sinned and have fallen short of the glory of God." We all have done wrong. So isn't it interesting that self-control is the last adornment? Perhaps it may be the most difficult! Yet it is so true. We cannot have Self-control unless we have Gentleness, or Faithfulness, or Goodness, or Kindness, or Patience, or Peace, or Joy. Why? Because they all are rooted in the first, which is Love. Do you see what God is doing in this process? It's not a onetime experience. No, we're to grow as does a tree—ever growing into the likeness of Jesus as seen by our changed lives.

The Garland. A beautiful promise from the Old Testament reads: "God delights in His people. He festoons His plain folk with salvation garlands." *(Now weave the garland in the branches.)* Why garlands? That as the lace-like garland is woven amongst the branches on the Christmas tree, so too the One who brings these salvation garlands wraps and weaves His presence throughout our lives and is called the very breath of God, the Holy Spirit. What a delicate picture for such a powerful message! God's love letter to us says that the Holy Spirit was sent to be our Comforter, Teacher, and Healer. He brings health and healing to the bare and misshapen areas of our lives that are out of order. When we allow Him, the Holy Spirit brings continued salvation in and through every part of our lives, making each area whole, full, and flourishing—like the healthy pine standing in strength and beauty. Decorated with the ornaments of His character and dressed in His righteousness, this is how the Holy Spirit brings the Lord's provision that we might be dressed for our purpose—crowned with Himself and with His glory—much like . . .

The Star atop the Christmas tree. And so, as is tradition, we have the official crowning of the tree. *(Place the star on top of the tree.)* It is the last adornment to complete the design and tells us that first and foremost at the top of our lives should be the emanating glory of God. Our purpose is to glorify the Father, and in turn, His glory would shine over us with His protection, on us with His grace, in us with His gifting, and through us with the light of His power. Jesus is called the Bright and Morning Star. And just as the star over Bethlehem pointed the way to baby Jesus, we too can point the way to Jesus, the resurrected King.

The Lights. As Jesus said, "Let your light so shine before men that they may see your good works and glorify your Father in heaven." *(Plug in the Christmas lights.)* And so we stand, a symbol of hope in a dark world, decorated and adorned with the strength and beauty of all He is, pointing others to Him, giving glory to God. We too can have this testimony. This is *The Testimony of the Tree.*

The Small Promising Pine. Not everyone feels like the beautifully adorned tree. Look at this small sprig left to the elements of the cold world. This scraggly pine barely has any needles. And as you can see, the wind and the elements have beat on this poor little tree. People can feel the same way. Not by their own design, but the elements and environment have caused them to grow crooked as well. It's not a very striking thing to behold, that's for sure. This tree needs the loving touch of the Master, too. Its branches are not full and flourishing and marked by eternal life. Alone it stands. So we are without knowing our Creator. And so, a life left to itself, without Him, is the same as this tree, forlorn. It is not tall and true, and its trunk may be twisted, made crooked by the elements. This is how we stand until someone tells us the good news about God's amazing love. Many believe that God is real and that His sacrificial love is for all but do not know His unconditional love is there in acceptance with our forgiveness. And so they sit and remain in this state—unadorned and depleted. But the Word of God says, "The Lord takes pleasure in His people, and He will beautify the humble with salvation." So look . . . what's the one thing that's left on this tree that the storms of life cannot remove?

The Pinecones. This poor little tree is covered with pinecones. Let me ask you, what is a pinecone? Yes, it's a seed! God, the Creator of all things, before the foundations of the world, preplanned the "who" of you. He placed these hidden seeds of gifting within you that wait to be released. They proclaim your hidden potential and destiny. It says in Jeremiah, a book in the Old Testament, "'For I know the plans I have for you,' declares the Lord. 'Plans to prosper you and not harm you, plans to give you a hope and a future. And when you come to me and pray to me, when you seek me with all your heart, then I will be found by you,' declares the Lord."

You know what's amazing about this? Do you know how a pinecone releases its seeds? It is only when it's totally dry, or when it's consumed by fire. Only God can make something beautiful from the thirst of a depleted life or the fires of trauma. Nothing can take away the hope that God deposited in us.

Remember the passage . . . "A life devoted to things is a dead life, a stump; but a God-shaped life is a flourishing tree." So which tree do you feel more like? How is hope embraced? The Christmas story gives the answer. As the babe in the manger came, salvation has come. As the angels announced, hope is ours. And as the wise men bowed, we are invited to do the same. Christmas now calls.

A host of angels first marked the birth of the Christ Child one starry night as a celebration of the hope, health, and healing He would bring, proclaiming "peace on earth and goodwill toward men" in heavenly chorus. Now, you too can bring "goodwill toward men" by sharing the good news and the experience of the message of "The Testimony of the Tree" as well as *Grandma's Christmas Legacy, The Testimony of the Tree* with others both here and abroad.

We invite you to visit the website to learn more of "The Testimony of the Tree" story and vision at www.testimonyofthetree.org. Here is how you can bring Christmas to others!

- *Grandma's Christmas Legacy, the Testimony of the Tree* gift books are available at the online store to purchase and share with friends and other families.

- Book Casey Schutrop to come share for a large group gathering. Visit Testimony of the Tree website or go to www.wowministriesintl.org.

- Sponsor units of a "Testimony of the Tree Kit" to freely share the good news of "The Testimony of the Tree" experience both here and around the world. Along with the message of "The Testimony of the Tree," they will receive a colorful, freestanding cardstock Christmas tree complete with the decor to trim this tree and together experience through a new tradition "The Testimony of the Tree" message.

This interactive website also allows you to share your experience of *Grandma's Christmas Legacy, the Testimony of the Tree* and hear how others worldwide have made it their tradition as they gather. In the children's corner, kids can meet and share their stories and pictures with other children from around the world.